YOUR ATTITUDE OF GRATITUDE

Develop Simple Gratitude Skills for Better Living

Sensei Paul David

COPYRIGHT PAGE

Your Attitude of Gratitude: Develop Simple Gratitude Skills for Better Living, by Sensei Paul David, Copyright © 2020.

All rights reserved.
ISBN# 9781777191320

This book is not authorized for free distribution copying.

www.senseipublishing.com

@senseipublishing
#senseipublishing

Check Out Another Book In This Series Visit:

www.amazon.com/author/senseipauldavid

Get Our FREE Books Today!

Click & Share The Links Below

FREE Kids Books
lifeofbailey.senseipublishing.com
kidsonearth.senseipublishing.com

FREE Self-Development Book For Every Family
senseiselfdevelopment.senseipublishing.com

Join Our Publishing Journey!

If you would like to receive FUTURE FREE BOOKS, and get to know us better, please click www.senseipublishing.com and join our newsletter by entering your email address in the pop-up box.

Follow Our Blog: senseipauldavid.ca

Follow/Like/Subscribe: Facebook, Instagram, YouTube: @senseipublishing

Scan the QR Code with your phone or tablet

to follow us on social media: Like / Subscribe / Follow

Contents

Welcome 1

Breaking Down Negativity 7

Highlighting Gratitude 14

Challenge #1: The 7-Day Negativity Diet 23

Challenge #2: 30-Day Gratitude Round-Up 28

New Skills, New Habits, New Beginning 33

Today is Looking Good 39

References 51

Thank You

Before we dive in, I'd like to thank you for picking up this book. Your time is valuable, and I know there are many other similar books and courses out there that offer to help, but you chose to invest in mine and that means everything to me.

Now that you're here, and if you stick with me, I promise to make our time together valuable and worthwhile.

In the pages ahead, you will find some areas of information and practices more helpful than others - and that's great because as you apply what works best for you, you will benefit from an exciting transformation of character. Enjoy!

Welcome

"Let us rise up and be thankful, for if
we didn't learn a lot today, at least
we learned a little."
— Gautama Buddha

The word gratitude is a beautiful word for us to include in our lives and daily practices. It is derived from the Latin word *gratus*, which means "thankful, pleasing." Therefore, in its simplest expression to be grateful is to have an appreciation and express thankfulness. In my case, I am grateful that you have chosen to read this book. However, more than my gratitude to you should be your thankfulness to your own curiosity about this book's contents and how it may guide you in a meaningful way.

The journey of discovery is shared with you is one not everyone will attempt. Your interest sets you apart and through the process of improving one's self, nurturing and self-care naturally exist. Whether you walk away with a little or a lot, you will walk away with a changed perspective for the better.

You will grow a bit more aware, gaining an understanding of the skills to help you in all areas of your life.

Perhaps you'll begin to enjoy and appreciate newfound curiosity to go beyond the surface level of life. You'll grow willing to dive into what really crafts your life—your internal perspective on all matters, both from within and in the world around you. There is no better way to recognize some of life's most precious things, large and small, than from your attitude of gratitude.

Yes, the attitude of gratitude is a common expression, easily found today in many resources. Despite its popularity, my experiences have revealed a few people experience the bliss that comes with authentic gratitude. The primary reason for this is a lack of focus. It doesn't appear to be present in many people so they can see wonderful things for what they are worth…In each moment and with a present state of mind.

It is so easy to get distracted. There is a chance that as you read this warm welcome to you, your thoughts drifted off a time or two. This has become so common to many people that it is considered human nature. Such does not have to be the case; our human nature is what we make it out to be, which means we can make it one of focus and inward serenity. The world's chaos you may feel does not have to be at home within you.

Chaos often stems from negativity, which leads to heaviness; heavy thoughts and challenges focusing on the right things. Have you ever noticed this in your life? Most have. My ambitious, yet worthy aspiration, is to help you move past the negative and dense thoughts and toward what is brighter and lighter. When your attitude and gratitude work together, you will experience this.

With an attitude of gratitude, you are continually challenging yourself to bring joy into your reality.

This is important to you for many reasons. A few that may be of interest to you include

- more balanced perspectives of situations in your life;
- stronger personal relationships;
- recognition of positive forces in your life;
- less stress;
- and better emotional and physical wellness.

The study conducted for the Greater Goods Science Center for John Templeton University and titled The Science of Gratitude[2] also notes how gratitude can vary depending on age, gender, and even nationality. Expressions of gratitude were also impactful when it came to recovery from certain mental and physical disorders. The benefits mentioned are worth your investment of time so you can gain an understanding of your starting point. This is where I come in and want to help. So, come as you are into this journey and know that if attention span and focus are your challenges, what is being shared is done so with you in mind.

This is what you will need as you go through the pages of this book:

- Curiosity: you want to learn more about how you can tap into an attitude of gratitude that serves you well in life. The bonus is how a better you can be of service to others.
- A compelling purpose to follow through: by having something in specific to inspire you to use this information to spark change, you will be more connected with your "why" in taking on the ideas, information, and challenges in this book. Some examples of compelling purposes are
    - children and grandchildren;
    - spouses and friends;
    - career goals and ambitions;
    - a need for better emotional health;
    - a need for better physical health;
    - a recharge of a life that feels dull and weighed down.

You are never too old or too young to discover the beauty of gratitude in your life. In fact, in a research paper listed on the NCBI website titled

Preschool-aged children's understanding of gratitude: Relations with emotion and mental state knowledge1, it states: "Children with a better early understanding of emotions and mental states understand more about gratitude." This is a reminder of how habits we develop as a child can carry us into adulthood without us being fully aware of it. As an adult, you can act to change this. Better yet, you can help children be connected to gratitude from their earliest formative years.

- A calendar (paper or phone): in order to monitor and track changes, a calendar is required. All of us have heard how "time flies by." We must also remember sentiments such as what psychologist Philip Zimbardo says: "Time matters because we are finite because time is the medium in which we live our lives."
- A notebook: taking notes of what stands out to you in this book is going to be relevant to how you track your progress. Rather than think, where was that again, write it down. This will also help to reinforce what stands out to you and incorporate a stronger memory recognition. Hand to paper is a powerful way to develop new habits.

This opportunity should feel exciting, promising. Remembering how it is designed to help you grow

with short and effective exercises helps take the pressure off. If you commit to the time to start, you will find it easy to follow through all the way to the end.
Congratulations on starting this and enjoy the process.

Sensei Paul

Breaking Down Negativity

"I will not let anyone walk through
my mind with their dirty feet."
— Mahatma Gandhi

Negativity is a powerful force to deal with. Once it becomes dominant it grows even stronger. Addressing it, in whatever form it may come to you, is important. It appears to us through:

- negative people around us,

    and,

- our own thoughts.

We are all able to shield ourselves from negative external forces while evicting that negativity we feel due to our own thoughts and actions.

In this chapter, negativity will be broken down so you can discover all the ways it currently impacts your life. There is a chance you've never taken the time to evaluate this before, which makes this information exciting, necessary, and perhaps a bit startling. Please remember, be gentle with yourself and understand why knowing is the starting point to change.

NEGATIVE BARRIERS

It may catch you off guard to acknowledge how negativity holds you back from the very things you want most in life. It works as a repellent for good and positive energy. Shifting away from this can only be beneficial to you.

Amy Morin, a clinical social worker, wrote an article for Psychology Today online titled *6 Bad Habits that Will Sabotage Your Success*[1]. In this article, she talks about putting yourself down and states: *"It's impossible to perform well when you're telling yourself 'You're stupid' or 'You can't ever do anything right.' Negative self-talk will discourage you from putting in your best effort and it will drag you down fast."*

Morin's advice on how to handle this: *"Stop the put-downs:* Talk to yourself like a trusted friend. If you wouldn't use such harsh words with someone else, don't allow your inner critic to say them to you."

A good chain effect happens when you stop being negative to yourself through your thoughts and actions. You create a boundary where you become less tolerant of others' negativity, thereby lessening it.

NEGATIVITY VERSUS ACHIEVEMENT

Whether a person has negative tendencies or not, they usually notice negativity in others. Here are some examples of how this internal dialogue or real-time conversation may sound like.

- I hope <insert name> doesn't come to the party. All they ever do is complain about <insert topic>.
- <Insert name> is so cranky. They must be a nightmare to work with.
- No matter what happens, I am going to avoid <insert name> as much as possible.

Have you ever heard one of these statements or a variation of one? Have you ever said something similar? These negative thoughts surface when we want to protect ourselves from those who overwhelm us with the way they communicate and presumably feel.

And when you are a person such as this, you are going to have thoughts comparable to these examples:

- I'll never get the job. They always pass me over.
- What's the point in saving up money? Some crazy and unexpected expense always comes up.

- I'm just destined to be alone.

Statements like what is listed here are all indicators of a life glitch that involves negative thinking. Thankfully, glitches can be fixed.

NEGATIVELY INFLUENCED RELATIONSHIPS

Relationships are the essence of life. They define our experiences, whether we are alone or with others. Negativity is one of the biggest influencers of the outcome of any relationship we have in our lives, both personal and professional.

Hiroko Akiyama et al. wrote a paper for The Journals of Gerontology titled *Negative Interactions in Close Relationships Across the Lifespan*[2]. In this paper, it is noted: "Close relationships can be positive and negative. They provide people with joy, comfort, and support. At the same time, they can be a source of conflict, frustration, and disappointment."

Akiyama further states: *"The literature suggests three plausible explanations for decreasing negativity in close relationships: maturity, familiarity, and contact frequency. The first explanation suggests that with increasing age people mature. They acquire social skills from experience, learn to control their emotions, and improve their emotional understanding."*

What makes this study particularly interesting is that more positive relationships seem to exist in people who learned to develop good relationships prior to the inundation of technologies such as social media. Yes, social media gets picked on much of the time but there are links to show its impact on negativity and relationships that cannot be ignored.

When you think of your life, think of how nice it would be to live by—and show others—how to thrive in positive relationships. This is a life-shifting change that creates a ripple of positivity.

THE STRESS FACTOR

If you desire to manage your stress, you will need to create a mix of habits and thought patterns geared toward stress management. This means you need to build up

- resilience,
- gratitude,
- and focus.

In addition, you need to evaluate your environment in its entirety, including personal habits, friends, and family. Do you spend free time indulging in the negative instead of accentuating the positive? Determine this and you may find the source of stress.

Also, the type of work you do can impact stress. Some pleasing news is that even if you find your work unrewarding, there is a way to be at peace with it and still feel the impact of positive thoughts in a work environment, more than negative responses.

The key to all this working for you is to commit to releasing anxieties and stressors when they do not help you live in a more positive manner.

PERSONAL INVENTORY

With all the access to the information we have, it is easy to want to evaluate ourselves. This is not always beneficial but when it comes to personal habits—such as negativity's influence in our life—self-evaluation is required. Embrace this process.

Every one of us has negative habits in our lives. The ones who don't allow themselves to get blocked by these habits are the ones who put steps in place to keep them in check.

It's time to put some thought into the negative habits you may have. If you are reading this from a book, you can feel free to write in the spaces below. Or, just like the digital book holders will do, use a notebook to write down all the steps you are taking as you work on this worthwhile task.

The negative habits impacting me most are:

1. _____
2. _____
3. _____
4. _____

5. _____
6. _____

Upon reflection, how does it make you feel when you use your negative habits on yourself and others, both intentionally and unintentionally?

_____
_____
_____
_____
_____

STATEMENT OF UNDERSTANDING

For our purposes, the statement of understanding for all the exercises in this book is a simple sentence or two to relay what you have learned and what you hope to adjust in your behavior to better connect with an attitude of gratitude.

Here's an example of a statement of understanding that applies to this chapter:

I am disheartened that I don't have a meaningful intimate relationship in my life, enough so that when I see someone else happy I go out of my way to cast negative thoughts toward them. This has an undesirable impact on me and I am ready to change this.

Now, you write down your statement of understanding about one or more of your negative thought patterns/habits. This will help you become aware of what may be worthy of you to work toward.

_____
_____

Highlighting Gratitude

"We need to learn to want what we
have, not to have what we want, in
order to get stable and steady
happiness."
— The Dalai Lama

One of the most beautiful things to hear, speak, and feel is a sentiment of gratitude. Positive feelings emit from this experience that can often carry a person through their entire day with more grace and dignity. Why would you choose to not seek out feeling this way daily, or at least as much as possible?

Gratitude's Helping Hand

This is something, author unknown, found on an online meme. It is a wonderful example of how gratitude is a helping hand for all of us in our day when we invite it in.

> **You've got to start romanticizing your life.**
> **See your commute to work as cute and fun.**
> **Make every cup of coffee you've ever had the best one**
> **you've ever had. Make small, mundane things exciting and new.**
> **When you do these things you truly start living; you look forward to every day.**

With gratitude, you will find you achieve more because you are mentally aligning yourself with

- better physical and psychological health;
- more empathy and less aggression;
- increased mental strength (resilience);
- and better sleep.

Most challenges people face come amidst a poor night's rest. In the article by Linda Wasmer Andrews titled *How Gratitude Helps You Sleep at Night*[1], found at Psychology Today online, she shares this research:

"Psychologists Robert Emmons and Michael McCullough asked people with neuromuscular

*disorders to make nightly lists of things for which they were grateful. After three weeks, participants reported getting longer, more refreshing sleep.
"Following up on this lead, researchers at the University of Manchester in England looked at how gratitude might affect people's snooze time. Their study included over 400 adults of all ages— 40% with sleep disorders—who completed questionnaires that asked about gratitude, sleep, and pre-sleep thoughts. Gratitude was related to having more positive thoughts, and fewer negative ones, at bedtime. This, in turn, was associated with dozing off faster and sleeping longer and better.
"In short, when you cultivate gratitude throughout the day, you're more likely to have positive thoughts as you're drifting off to sleep. Rather than ruminating over the friend who forgot to call, you're thinking of the coworker who stayed late to help you. Instead of obsessing over bills, you're thinking of the new client you just landed. With positive thoughts as a lullaby, you're more likely to drift off into a peaceful slumber."*
Health, stress, happiness, and achievement all have common threads between them which link gratitude to wellness. The two challenges you'll be doing in this book will work directly with this. The exciting thing is, they can be used effectively and in an age appropriate way, incorporating your entire family (and even workplace) into making positivity the habit of choice.

THE ROLE OF GRATITUDE IN OUR RELATIONSHIPS

Gratitude plays a valuable role in cultivating and maintaining peoples' relationships, in all areas of their lives. According to a paper presented by The Greater Good Science Center at UC Berkeley[2], regarding intimate relationships:
"Receiving a thoughtful benefit from a partner was followed by increased feelings of gratitude and indebtedness. While men in the couple reported more mixed emotions than did women, experiencing more gratitude from these acts of kindness predicted both partners feeling more connected and satisfied with their relationship the next day."
Additionally, noted in this same paper:
"A subsequent study asked some participants to express gratitude more frequently to a friend or romantic partner; other participants were asked to focus on their daily activities, increase their grateful thoughts about their partner, or focus on positive memories that included their partner. The researchers found that, compared to the other participants, those who expressed more gratitude toward a romantic partner or close friend at one time point reported greater comfort in voicing relationship concerns in the future, and that expressing gratitude more often led to more positive perceptions of a friend, which in turn led the participants to be more comfort-able voicing relationship concerns. These findings might have

therapeutic implications, as they suggest that expressing more gratitude to a partner or friend may nurture other skills that help improve relationships, such as making people feel more comfortable discussing potential relationship conflicts."

Through finding better ways to use gratitude in our intimate relationships, we are also learning valuable skills to take out into the world and connect positively with all life relationships.

Stress "Less"

Just as negativity can elevate stress, gratitude can reduce it. When we remember all the things there are to appreciate in this world, it becomes significantly easier to savor the small things and keep a "reality check" of our lives that are rooted in goodness. Life becomes less focused on what may possibly go wrong and more appreciative of all that is good.

A nice way to help manage stress is to think about lessening it one day at a time. We can only manage what we are given in a day, which makes it quite logical to choose to dwell on what we are grateful for over what we are concerned about. This doesn't mean we don't address concerns and problems. It refers to spending time on our stressful problems from the healthier mental perspective that comes with gratitude.

GRATITUDE'S RIPPLE EFFECT

The carryover effects of gratitude are easy to correlate to sentiments from people who volunteer their time: they feel the rewards of what they've contributed as much as those who received their time and attention benefit. How incredible!

What we do to improve our own lives has the potential to have a profound and positive impact on another's life too.

Dr. Martin E. P. Seligman is a psychologist at the University of Pennsylvania. He tested the impact of various positive psychology interventions on 411 people, each compared with a control assignment of writing about early memories. This was one of their assignments, as noted in a Harvard Health Publishing study for Harvard Medical School[3]: *"When their week's assignment was to write and personally deliver a letter of gratitude to someone who had never been properly thanked for his or her kindness, participants immediately exhibited a huge increase in happiness scores. This impact was greater than that from any other intervention, with benefits lasting for a month."*

Take a few minutes and imagine how you might change a life by doing something similar. This is a wonderful, simple-to-do activity that even the smallest child can participate in. Perhaps they draw a picture for someone they are grateful for instead of writing a letter.

PERSONAL INVENTORY

Robert Brault penned: "Enjoy the little things, for one day you may look back and realize they were the big things." This sentiment states the intent of this personal inventory exercise. It is meant to be an enjoyable process for you to dive into what you may be grateful for in your life, from small to large. You'll want to focus on the habits you have in expressing these things, evaluating if you show gratitude

- automatically,
- with heart,
- at certain times of day,
- to create a favorable shift to your mood,
- or in other ways not mentioned here.

If you don't have many of these habits currently feel free to write down when you see yourself using gratitude. You know more about an attitude of gratitude now than you may have just a short time ago.

My gratitude habits are:

1. _____
2. _____
3. _____

4. _____
5. _____
6. _____

Upon reflection, I am aware of how I use gratitude habits in my daily life. This is how these habits impact me and others, both intentionally and unintentionally.

_____
_____
_____
_____
_____
_____

STATEMENT OF UNDERSTANDING

It's time to connect personal meaning to the information you've learned about gratitude habits. Here is an example of how a statement of understanding for this chapter may look:
One of my most cherished times of day happens right away in the morning when I wake up. As I stretch and welcome the day, I think of all my blessings, including my comfy pillow and even the gentle breathing of those I love who are still sound asleep.

_____

_____
_____
_____
_____
_____

Your warm and appreciative thought is one you can use to keep you centered and focused on gratitude's importance.

Challenge #1: The 7-Day Negativity Diet

"Negativity is cannibalistic. The more you feed it, the bigger and stronger it grows."
— Bobby Darnell

A negativity diet will leave you feeling fuller and more satisfied than you've possibly felt in a long while. And like most diets, it'll be easy for the first day, then there will be a few tough days, and then it will grow easier again. Only, in our case, instead of craving food, it's resisting negative thoughts.

Our brains are tricky. They constantly bombard us with negative thoughts. Why? Mostly because we've let them get away with doing that to us for a long time. So, like a stubborn person, the brain resists change until we wear it down.

The eventual result of a negativity diet is that positivity takes over, and that is exactly what you want your brain to respond to.

HOW THE 7-DAY NEGATIVITY DIET WORKS

This is one of the easiest diets to understand—which gives you something to be grateful for immediately.

Everything you do this week is going to focus on one thing: eliminating negative thoughts. This includes

- in what you say,
- in what you do,
- and in how you act.

If a negative thought surfaces, you will be prepared to safeguard yourself against it by

- interrupting your attention,
- keeping your mouth shut,
- and relaying a grateful thought.

You can do these things!

MAKING IT PAST THE NEGATIVITY HUNGER PAINS

The action you will take if you're craving a taste of negativity will include discovering the: 1) how; 2) why; and 3) when.

1. *How*

    How did you get to this negative moment? Perhaps it was a trigger from something another person said or an event that happened to you. Take some time to think of how the negativity crept in right away so you can stop it from creeping in further.

2. *Why*

Why would you be compelled to spend your energy on this negative thought? There are few (if any) examples of when spending extensive time dwelling in negativity has produced anything positive. Contrary, when using positive means to deal with what's negative, you can dissolve or solve situations and not carry their heavy weight in your being.

3. When

When does negativity seem to sneak up on you? Depending on your personality, this could happen at a typical time like it does for most people (hungry, tired, stressed, etc.) or it could happen at unexpected times (ex: your kid smarting off to you, a fight with your spouse, someone cutting you off in traffic). It's up to you to step up to your defense and know when it's happening so you can counteract negativity right away.

By following through with your 7-Day Negativity Diet, you are going to feel so much better—mentally and emotionally lighter. Once you feel this way, it's a place of betterment you'll want to remain in touch with.

YOUR DIET DETAILS

Now it's time to write down your plans so you can be prepared to go on a healthy mental diet to clean out negativity.

- Write down the date you want to start your 7-Day Negativity Diet: _____

- Write down the date it will be in 7 days: _____

- Write down how you will go about being steadfast in your negativity diet: _____
  _____
  _____
  _____
  _____
  _____

- If you struggle with your 7-Day Negativity Diet and fail at first, are you willing to start over?
  _____
  _____

_____
_____
_____

(If your answer isn't "yes," find a way to commit to a "yes.")

STATEMENT OF UNDERSTANDING

I will benefit from this 7-Day Negativity Diet most by
_____
_____
_____
_____
_____
_____

CHALLENGE #2: 30-DAY GRATITUDE ROUND-UP

"Feeling gratitude and not expressing it is like wrapping a present and not giving it." — William Arthur Ward

If this challenge was a billboard, it would be a simple one: 30 Days to Your Attitude of Gratitude.

HOW THE 30-DAY GRATITUDE ROUND-UP WORKS

The results of this challenge are fantastic, and it is very easy to do. All you need is either you or another person, and a minute of your time committed to the round-up every day, for 30 days. Here is what you are going to do:

1. Ask yourself or someone else what they are grateful for. Do this in the morning so you can carry the spirit of gratitude around with you.
2. Write down what you or the person is grateful for in your notebook. See the beauty in appreciating the moment. Smile and breathe in as you absorb the positive thought.
3. Review this at least once every 10 days. Mark it down on your phone if you need to. When

doing the review, take time to appreciate the variety of things you or others are thankful for.

Please note, with this exercise, you are encouraged to incorporate others into it, although it is not required. The reason this is a good idea is that you can already begin to spread the idea of gratitude to someone else, which is a reinforcement for you. Additionally, in turn, others may keep gratitude's positive energy moving in their own lives, and in others.

It's Round-Up Time

A common setback people have about incorporating others into the 30-Day Gratitude Round-Up is that they feel awkward asking others what they are grateful for. This is understandable and will feel uncomfortable the first few times you do it if you've never done it before. If this is you, remember these things to help assure you that all is well:

- Sometimes people struggle more when they try to find an answer within themselves than they do asking someone else.
- People like opportunities to talk about what's nice in their lives. Some people, believe it or not, feel it is bragging to express gratitude so they keep these thoughts to themselves.

However, expressing gratitude isn't bragging because every person in this world has something to be grateful for and they can set an example for someone else on how gratitude works.

> **TIP: If you come across a person who shrugs or cannot give you a sincere answer, just smile and move on.**

Here are a few people you may want to consider asking about what they are grateful for:

- Spouse or partner
- Children
- Co-worker
- Random person (if you're brave—maybe coffee house line)
- Your driver (bus, Uber, Lyft, etc.)
- Postal person
- Cashier

Everyone is somebody you can ask if you feel comfortable doing so. An interesting observation that has been noted is many people find the opportunities to ask about gratitude start to come naturally—without a second thought—as they incorporate it into their day. Are you the next person to recognize this?

REALIZING YOUR BENEFITS

A few of the benefits of this exercise have already been laid out in this book. One example would be making gratitude a positive habit in your day. This is the goal in the end; to recognize all that you can to be grateful for, even in your life's crazier moments.
Additionally, after 30 days is up, you are going to feel other positive side effects, including:

- Enthusiasm to evaluate gratitude every morning
- Ideas on how to further incorporate gratitude throughout your day
- More smiles because you have much to be grateful for
- A better outlook on life
- More energy to draw the attention of the right kinds of conversations, opportunities, and people
- Less stress and tension
- An openness to find creative solutions to make other types of changes in your life

This challenge is a win/win. What's also exciting about it is how it's an easy habit to get kids into early on. Imagine this:

Your small child is in the cart in the grocery store line and the cashier's scanning through your purchases. Your child asks the cashier: "What are you grateful for today?" The cashier is surprised and then smiles. Maybe answering something like: "Meeting such a nice kid like you."

Do you think that the cashier would share what happened with someone else? They likely would, because it felt good and it's memorable — rare (although hopefully becoming more commonplace).

STATEMENT OF UNDERSTANDING

I am excited to benefit from my 30-Day Gratitude Round-Up by

_____
_____
_____

NEW SKILLS, NEW HABITS, NEW BEGINNING

"Depending on what they are, our
habits will either make us or break us.
We become what we repeatedly do."
— Sean Covey

The commitment to develop new skills and habits can be challenging in many cases. Mostly because the rewards are not always immediate. With establishing an attitude of gratitude that lasts, you have an edge because it

- doesn't take a lot of time,
- it's not complex,
- and you feel internal rewards rather quickly.

With most habit development, the reward seems to be the key to its success. With poor habits, the rewards can be immediate (smoking or comfort food, for example). Good habits sometimes take longer—practicing gratitude being an exception. Please accept the wonderful opportunity you have here for what it is. Take advantage of the wisdom and steps to a new beginning that is being shared next. Enjoy the process.

3 Nuggets of Wisdom to Guide You

Creating a new skill or habit doesn't come instantly. Although simple and ideal for those who are lacking focus, even creating an attitude of gratitude will require a commitment from you. Allow these 3 nuggets of wisdom to guide you.

1. Acknowledge that human nature naturally does what it must do, not what it should do. This means that we are often in survival mode, only thinking of an immediate result over a long-term benefit. Therefore, a commitment is needed to look beyond the "immediate" and into the betterment of your future.
2. Recognize a habit can take a bit of time to form. This happens for several reasons, including how challenging the habit is the amount of effort you put into the change and the mindset and frame of experiences you have in the beginning. All people are different in the amount of time it takes to develop a habit or new skill. Your calling is to focus on your growth—it's not a race against others.
3. Set up a calendar for your attitude of gratitude commitment for at least 6 months. This will

give you ample time to act, reflect, and recognize the benefits you are receiving. This is the inspiration that can keep you going until the habit is formed. It's also worth noting that inspiration is different than motivation. Motivation typically lasts about a day. Inspiration has the potential to last a lifetime.

By following these nuggets of wisdom you'll find yourself being more diligent and kinder to yourself. There is no downside to this!

3 STEPS TO A NEW BEGINNING

Take the time to reflect on the possibilities of what could exist with a stronger presence of gratitude in your life. Make a difference by making a commitment to these 3 steps.

1. Think of everything you stand to lose over the next years if you do not make a shift in your mindset to one of positivity and gratitude. Ask yourself these questions:

   a. Do I feel the goodness of life today?

   b. How do I help others feel gratitude and appreciation?

   c. Would I want to hang around me for a day if I just met myself, as is?

2. Create a clear picture of what your life is like with more gratitude in it. Ask yourself these questions:

    a. How do I desire to feel when I wake up in the morning?

    b. What does it feel like to give or receive a genuine smile of gratitude?

    c. What benefits will I receive from practicing gratitude consistently?

3. Make your commitment and "seal the deal" by stating this out loud: "I am a grateful person." Do this in the present tense each day to remind yourself. There is no limit on how often you can do this, either. Whatever it takes is yours for the taking. Think of how much a musician practices to master their instrument. This also requires practice and it is achievable by all. What makes you special for doing this is your commitment to it, as not everyone has it.

These 3 steps will get you going; the way you feel will keep you flowing into your attitude of gratitude.

> **TIP: This is an invitation to meditation to help you make shifts to**

your mindset. Feel free to take advantage of the guided meditation practices I've created for you by visiting or downloading the app: 'Insight Timer' and searching for or clicking this link Sensei Paul David. You'll find a variety of meditations, both for adults and with a focus on children.

STATEMENT OF UNDERSTANDING

My attitude of gratitude is worth my commitment because:

_____
_____
_____
_____

TODAY IS LOOKING GOOD

"I am tomorrow, or some future day, what I establish today. I am today what I established yesterday or some previous day."
— James Joyce

May you feel as excited about this life opportunity for yourself as I feel for you. You're on the cusp of making a transition for the better. You've gained an understanding of information about:

- The consequences in your life caused by negativity
- Ways that gratitude can enhance your life, as well as the lives of those around you
- An exciting vision of how gratitude can play out in your life
- Practical steps and strategies to help you create the habits and skills it takes to gain your attitude of gratitude

To help you learn how to accomplish an authentic, now-a-part-of-you, gratitude practice, you can implement the challenges laid out for you.

- Challenge #1: The 7-Day Negativity Diet

- Challenge #2: The 30-Day Gratitude Round-Up

You've also learned why you want to have an attitude of gratitude. Because of this, you know that it is a pursuit worth remaining on for as long as you need.

It's a great day to be alive! And I thank you for your commitment to gratitude and a better approach to all you partake in.

Everyone is invited join our creative journey! Please like/follow/share/subscribe on:

Instagram/Facebook @senseipublishing

YouTube or Google #senseipublishing

We really appreciate the support. Thank You!

Life of Bailey: Copyright Reserved by

Paul David © 2020

ISBN: 9781777191320

Independently published

Scan using your phone/iPad camera for Social Media

Thank you for reading this book!

If you found this book helpful, I would be grateful if you would post an honest review on Amazon so this book can reach and help other people.

All you need to do is to visit amazon.com/author/senseipauldavid click the correct book cover, and click on the blue link next to the yellow stars that says, "customer reviews."

As always... It's a great day to be alive!

Check Out Another Book In This Series Visit:

www.amazon.com/author/senseipauldavid

www.senseipublishing.com

@senseipublishing
#senseipublishing

Check out our **recommendations** for other books for adults & kids plus other

great resources by visiting
www.senseipublishing.com/resources/

Join Our Publishing Journey!

If you would like to receive FREE BOOKS, special offers, please visit www.senseipublishing.com and join our newsletter by entering your email address in the pop-up box, and

Follow Our Engaging Blog NOW! senseipauldavid.ca

Get Our FREE Books Today!

Click & Share the Links Below

FREE Kids Books
lifeofbailey.senseipublishing.com
kidsonearth.senseipublishing.com

FREE Self-Development Book

senseiselfdevelopment.senseipublishing.com

FREE BONUS!!!
Experience Over 25 FREE Engaging Guided Meditations!

Prized Skills & Practices for Adults & Kids. Help Restore Deep-Sleep, Lower Stress, Improve Posture, Navigate Uncertainty & More.

Download the Free Insight Timer App and click the link below:
http://insig.ht/sensei_paul

If you like these meditations & want to go deeper email me for a FREE 30min LIVE Coaching Session:
senseipauldavid@senseipublishing.com

About the Author

I create simple & transformative eBooks & Guided Meditations for Adults & Children proven to help navigate uncertainty, solve niche problems & bring families closer together.

I'm a former finance project manager, private pilot, jiu-jitsu instructor, musician & former University of Toronto Fitness Trainer. I prefer a science-based approach to focus on these & other areas in my life to stay humble & hungry to evolve. I hope you enjoy my work and I'd love to hear your feedback.

- It's a great day to be alive!
Sensei Paul David

Scan & Follow/Like/Subscribe:
Facebook, Instagram, YouTube:
@senseipublishing

Scan using your phone/iPad camera for Social Media

Visit us at www.senseipublishing.com and sign up to our newsletter to learn more about our exciting books and to experience our FREE Guided Meditations for Kids & Adults.

REFERENCES

Invitation: if you are interested to dive deeper into any of the information shared, here are the resources where details were found.

INTRODUCTION

[1] Jackie A. Nelson, et al., Preschool-aged children's understanding of gratitude: Relations with emotion and mental state knowledge, March 28, 2012, extracted from:
https://www.ncbi.nlm.nih.gov/pmc/articles/PMC5224866/
on January 6, 2020.

[2] Summer Allen, Ph.D., The Science of Gratitude: A white paper prepared for the John Templeton Foundation by the Greater Good Science Center at UC Berkeley, May 2018, extracted from:
https://ggsc.berkeley.edu/images/uploads/GGSC-JTF_White_Paper-Gratitude-FINAL.pdf
on January 20, 2020.

BREAKING DOWN NEGATIVITY

[1] Amy Morin, 6 Bad Habits that Will Sabotage Your Success, Psychology Today online, March 3, 2016, extracted from:
https://www.psychologytoday.com/us/blog/what-mentally-strong-people-dont-do/201603/6-bad-habits-will-sabotage-your-success on January 6, 2020.

[2] Hiroko Akiyama et al, Negative Interactions in Close Relationships Across the Lifespan, The Journals of Gerontology, *Series B*, Volume 58, Issue 2, March 2003, Pages P70–P79, extracted from:

https://academic.oup.com/psychsocgerontology/article/58/2/P70/557810 on January 6, 2020.

HIGHLIGHTING GRATITUDE

[1] Linda Wasmer Andrews, How Gratitude Helps You Sleep at Night, Psychology Today online, November 9, 2011, extracted from:
https://www.psychologytoday.com/us/blog/minding-the-body/201111/how-gratitude-helps-you-sleep-night
extracted on January 6, 2020.

[2] Summer Allen, Ph.D., The Science of Gratitude: A white paper prepared for the John Templeton Foundation by the Greater Good Science Center at UC Berkeley, May 2018, extracted from:
https://ggsc.berkeley.edu/images/uploads/GGSC-JTF_White_Paper-Gratitude-FINAL.pdf on January 6, 2020.

[3] In Praise of Gratitude, Harvard Mental Health Letter, June 5, 2019, Harvard Health Publishing: Harvard Medical School, extracted from:
https://www.health.harvard.edu/mind-and-mood/in-praise-of-gratitude on January 6, 2020.

www.ingramcontent.com/pod-product-compliance
Lightning Source LLC
LaVergne TN
LVHW051226070526
838200LV00057B/4629